The Federal Re

Dean Henderson

The Federal Reserve Cartel
Dean Henderson

"There is no such thing as a free press. You know it and I know it. There's not one of you who would dare to write his honest opinions. The role of journalism is to destroy truth, to lie outright, to pervert, to fawn at the feet of Mammon...We are tools and vassals of the men behind the scenes. We are jumping jacks: they pull the strings, we dance; our talents, our possibilities and our lives are the property of these men. We are intellectual prostitutes"

John Swainton, Chief of Staff of the New York Times (1860-1870)

*For my ancestors and for the emancipation
of all creatures of this Earth.*

The Eight Families

The Four Horsemen of US Banking – Chase Manhattan, Citigroup, Bank of America and Wells Fargo - own the Four Horsemen of Oil, in tandem with Goldman Sachs, Deutsche Bank, *Banque Paribas*, Barclays and other European old money behemoths. But their monopoly over the global economy does not stop at the edge of the oil patch. According to company 10K filings to the SEC, these same Four Horsemen of Banking are also among the top 10 stock holders of virtually every Fortune 500 corporation. [1]

So who then are the stockholders in these money center banks? This information is guarded closely. Queries to bank regulatory agencies regarding stock ownership in the top 25 US bank holding companies are given Freedom of Information Act status, after which information regarding ownership of the banks is denied on national security grounds. This is rather ironic, since many of the bank's stockholders reside in Europe.

One important repository for the wealth of the global oligarchy which own these bank holding companies is US Trust Corporation, founded in 1853. As of 1995, US Trust's Corporate Director and Honorary Trustee was Walter Rothschild. Other directors include Daniel Davison of JP Morgan Chase, Richard Tucker of Exxon Mobil, Daniel Roberts of Citigroup and Marshall Schwartz of Morgan Stanley. [2]

J. W. McCallister, oil industry insider with House of Saud connections, wrote in *The Grim Reaper* that information he acquired from Saudi bankers cited 80% ownership of the New York Federal Reserve Bank - by far the most powerful Fed branch - by just eight families, only four of which reside in the US. They are the Goldman Sachs, Rockefellers, Lehmans and Kuhn Loebs of New York; the Rothschilds of Paris and London; the Warburgs of Hamburg; the Lazards of Paris; and the Israel Moses Seifs of Rome.

CPA Thomas D. Schauf corroborates McCallister's claims, adding that ten banks control all twelve Federal Reserve Bank branches. He names N.M. Rothschild of London, Rothschild Bank of Berlin, Warburg Bank of Hamburg, Warburg Bank of Amsterdam, Lehman Brothers of New York, Lazard Brothers of

Paris, Kuhn Loeb Bank of New York, Israel Moses Seif Bank of Italy, Goldman Sachs of New York and JP Morgan Chase Bank of New York. Schauf lists William Rockefeller, Paul Warburg, Jacob Schiff and James Stillman as individuals who own huge shares of the Fed. [3] The Schiffs are insiders at Kuhn Loeb. The Stillmans are Citibank powerhouses, who married into the Rockefeller clan at the turn of the century.

Eustace Mullins came to the same conclusions in his book *The Secrets of the Federal Reserve*, in which he displays charts connecting the Fed and its member banks to the families of Rothschild, Warburg, Rockefeller and the others. [4] The control that these banking families exert over the global economy cannot be overstated and is quite intentionally shrouded in secrecy. Their corporate media arm is quick to discredit any information exposing these money powers as half-baked conspiracy theory. The word "conspiracy" itself has been demonized, much like the word "communism". Anyone who dare utter the word is quickly excluded from public debate and written off as insane. Yet the facts remain.

The House of Morgan

The Federal Reserve Bank was born in 1913, the same year US banking scion J. Pierpont Morgan died and the Rockefeller Foundation was formed. The House of Morgan presided over American finance from the corner of Wall Street and Broad, acting as quasi-US central bank since 1838, when George Peabody founded it in London. Peabody was a business associate of the Rothschilds. In 1952 Fed researcher Eustace Mullins put forth the supposition that the Morgans were nothing more than Rothschild agents. Mullins wrote that the Rothschilds, "...preferred to operate anonymously in the US behind the facade of J.P. Morgan & Company"[5] Author Gabriel Kolko states, "Morgan's activities in 1895-1896 in selling US gold bonds in Europe were based on an alliance with the House of Rothschild."[6]

Morgan Grenfell operated in London. *Morgan et Ce* ruled Paris. The Rothschild's Lambert cousins set up Drexel & Company in Philadelphia. The House of Morgan catered to the Astors,

DuPonts, Guggenheims, Vanderbilts and Rockefellers. It financed the launch of AT&T, General Motors, General Electric and DuPont. Like the London-based Rothschild and Barings banks, Morgan became part of the power structure in many countries.

By 1890 the House of Morgan was lending to Egypt's central bank, financing Russian railroads, floating Brazilian provincial government bonds and funding Argentine public works projects. A recession in 1893 enhanced Morgan's power. That year Morgan saved the US government from a bank panic, forming a syndicate to prop up government reserves with a shipment of $62 million worth of Rothschild gold. [7]

Morgan was the driving force behind Western expansion in the US, financing and controlling West-bound railroads through voting trusts. In 1879 Cornelius Vanderbilt's New York Central Railroad gave preferential shipping rates to John D. Rockefeller's Standard Oil. The Rockefeller/Morgan relationship was cemented. The House of Morgan was now under Rothschild and Rockefeller family control. A *New York Herald* headline read, "Railroad Kings Form Gigantic Trust". J. Pierpont Morgan, who once stated, "Competition is a sin", now opined gleefully, "Think of it. All competing railroad traffic west of St. Louis placed in the control of about thirty men."[8]

Morgan and Edward Harriman's banker Kuhn Loeb held a monopoly over the railroads, while banking dynasties Lehman, Goldman Sachs and Lazard joined the Rockefellers in controlling the US industrial base. [9] In 1903 Banker's Trust was set up by the Eight Families. Benjamin Strong of Banker's Trust soon became the first Governor of the New York Federal Reserve Bank. The 1913 creation of the Fed fused the power of the Eight Families to the military and diplomatic might of the US government. If overseas debt went unpaid, the oligarchs could now deploy US Marines to collect their money. Morgan, Chase and Citibank soon formed an international lending syndicate.

The House of Morgan was cozy with the British House of Windsor and the Italian House of Savoy. The Kuhn Loebs, Warburgs, Lehmans, Lazards, Israel Moses Seifs and Goldman Sachs also had close ties to European royalty. By 1895 Morgan controlled the flow of gold in and out of the US. The first American wave of mergers was in its infancy and was being promoted by the bankers. In 1897 there were sixty-nine industrial mergers. By 1899 there were twelve-hundred.

In 1904 John Moody - founder of Moody's Investor Services - said it was impossible to talk of Rockefeller and Morgan interests as separate. [10] Public distrust of the combine spread. Many considered them traitors working for European old money. Rockefeller's Standard Oil, Andrew Carnegie's US Steel and Edward Harriman's railroads were all financed by banker Jacob Schiff at Kuhn Loeb, who worked closely with the European Rothschilds.

Several Western states banned the bankers. Populist preacher William Jennings Bryan was narrowly defeated in his underdog run at the US Presidency in 1896. The central theme of Bryan's campaign was that America was falling into a trap of "financial servitude to British capital". His rival President Teddy Roosevelt was forced by this spreading populist wildfire to enact tough anti-trust legislation, including the Sherman Anti-Trust Act.

In 1912 the Pujo hearings were held, addressing concentration of power on Wall Street. That same year Mrs. Edward Harriman sold her substantial shares in New York's Guaranty Trust Bank to J.P. Morgan, creating Morgan Guaranty Trust. Judge Louis Brandeis convinced President Woodrow Wilson to call for an end to interlocking board directorates. In 1914 the Clayton Anti-Trust Act was passed.

Jack Morgan - J. Pierpont's son and successor - responded by calling on Morgan clients Remington and Winchester to increase arms production. He argued that the US needed to enter WWI. Goaded by the Carnegie Foundation and other oligarchy fronts, Wilson accommodated. As Charles Tansill wrote in *America Goes to War*, "Even before the clash of arms, the French firm of Rothschild Freres cabled to Morgan & Company in New York suggesting the flotation of a loan of $100 million, a substantial part of which was to be left in the US to pay for French purchases of American goods."

The House of Morgan financed half the US war effort, while receiving commissions for lining up contractors like GE, Du Pont, US Steel, Kennecott and ASARCO. All were Morgan clients. Morgan had also financed the British Boer War in South Africa and the Franco-Prussian War. The 1919 Paris Peace Conference was presided over by Morgan, which led both German and Allied reconstruction efforts. [11]

In the 1930's populism resurfaced in America after Goldman Sachs, Lehman Bank and others profited from the Crash of 1929. [12] House Banking Committee Chairman Louis McFadden (D-NY) said of the Great Depression, "It was no accident. It was a carefully contrived occurrence...The international bankers sought to bring about a condition of despair here so they might emerge as rulers of us all".

Sen. Gerald Nye (D-ND) chaired a munitions investigation in 1936. Nye concluded that the House of Morgan had plunged the US into WWI to protect loans and create a booming arms industry. Nye later produced a document titled *The Next War*, which cynically referred to "the old goddess of democracy trick", through which Japan could be used to lure the US into WWII. In 1937 Interior Secretary Harold Ickes warned of the influence of "America's 60 Families". Historian Ferdinand Lundberg penned a book of the exact same title. Supreme Court Justice William O. Douglas decried, "Morgan influence...the most pernicious one in industry and finance today."

Jack Morgan responded by nudging the US towards WWII. Morgan had close relations with the Iwasaki and Dan families, Japan's two wealthiest clans, who have owned Mitsubishi and Mitsui, respectively, since the companies emerged from 17th Century *shogunates*. When Japan invaded Manchuria, slaughtering Chinese peasants at Nanking, Morgan downplayed the incident. Morgan also had close relations with Italian fascist Benito Mussolini, while German Nazi Dr. Hjalmer Schacht was a Morgan Bank *liaison* during WWII. After the war Morgan representatives met with Schacht at the Bank of International Settlements (BIS) in Basel, Switzerland. [13]

The House of Rockefeller

BIS is the most powerful bank in the world, a global central bank for the Eight Families who control the private central banks of almost all Western and developing nations. The first President of BIS was Rockefeller banker Gates McGarrah - an official at Chase Manhattan and the Federal Reserve. McGarrah is the grandfather of former CIA director Richard Helms. The Rockefellers- like the Morgans- had close ties to London. David Icke writes in *Children of the Matrix*, that the Rockefellers and Morgans were just "gofers" for the European Rothschilds. [14]

BIS is owned by the Federal Reserve, Bank of England, Bank of Italy, Bank of Canada, Swiss National Bank, *Nederlandsche* Bank, *Bundesbank* and Bank of France. Historian Carroll Quigley says BIS was part of a plan, "to create a world system of financial control in private hands able to dominate the political system of each country and the economy of the world as a whole...to be controlled in a feudalistic fashion by the central banks of the world acting in concert by secret agreements."

The US government had a historical distrust of BIS, lobbying unsuccessfully for its demise at the 1944 post-WWII Bretton Woods Conference. Instead the Eight Families' power was exacerbated, with the Bretton Woods creation of the IMF and the World Bank. The US Federal Reserve only took shares in BIS in September 1994. [15] BIS holds at least 10% of monetary reserves for at least 80 of the world's central banks, the IMF and other multilateral institutions. It serves as financial agent for international agreements, collects information on the global economy and serves as lender of last resort to prevent global financial collapse.

BIS promotes an agenda of monopoly capitalist fascism. It gave a bridge loan to Hungary in the 1990's to ensure privatization of that country's economy. It served as conduit for Eight Families funding of Adolf Hitler - led by the Warburg's J. Henry Schroeder and Mendelsohn Bank of Amsterdam. Many researchers assert that BIS is at the nadir of global drug money laundering. [16] It is no coincidence that BIS is headquartered in Switzerland, favorite hiding place for the wealth of the global aristocracy and headquarters for P-2 Alpina Lodge and Nazi International. Other institutions which the

Eight Families control include the World Economic Forum, the International Monetary Conference and the World Trade Organization.

Bretton Woods was a boon to the Eight Families. The IMF and World Bank were central to this "new world order". In 1944 the first World Bank bonds were floated by Morgan Stanley and First Boston. The French Lazard family became more involved in House of Morgan interests. Lazard Freres - France's biggest investment bank - is owned by the Lazard and David-Weill families - old Genoese banking scions represented by Michelle Davive. A recent Chairman and CEO of Citigroup was Sanford Weill.

In 1968 Morgan Guaranty launched Euro-Clear, a Brussels-based bank clearing system for Eurodollar securities. It was the first such automated endeavor. Some took to calling Euro-Clear "The Beast". Brussels serves as headquarters for the new European Central Bank and for NATO. In 1973 Morgan officials met secretly in Bermuda to illegally resurrect the old House of Morgan, twenty years *before* Glass Steagal Act was repealed. Morgan and the Rockefellers provided the financial backing for Merrill Lynch, boosting it into the Big Five of US investment banking. Merrill is now part of Bank of America.

John D. Rockefeller employed his oil wealth in acquiring Equitable Trust, which had gobbled up several large banks and corporations by the 1920's. The Great Depression helped consolidate Rockefeller's power. His Chase Bank merged with Kuhn Loeb's Manhattan Bank to form Chase Manhattan, cementing a long-time family relationship. The Kuhn-Loeb's had financed - along with Rothschilds - Rockefeller's quest to become king of the oil patch. National City Bank of Cleveland provided John D. with the money needed to embark upon his monopolization of the US oil industry. The bank was identified in Congressional hearings as being one of three Rothschild-owned banks in the US during the 1870's, when Rockefeller first incorporated as Standard Oil of Ohio. [17]

One Rockefeller Standard Oil partner was Edward Harkness, whose family came to control Chemical Bank. Another was James Stillman, whose family came to control Manufacturers Hanover Trust. Both banks are now part of JP Morgan Chase. Two of James

Stillman's daughters married two of William Rockefeller's sons. The two families control Citibank as well. [18]

In the insurance business, the Rockefellers control Metropolitan Life, Equitable Life, Prudential and New York Life. Rockefeller banks control 25% of all assets of the 50 largest US commercial banks and 30% of all assets of the 50 largest insurance companies. [19] Insurance companies - the first in the US was launched by Freemasons through their Woodman's of America - play a key role in the Bermuda drug money shuffle.

Companies under Rockefeller control include Exxon Mobil, Chevron Texaco, BP Amoco, Marathon Oil, Freeport McMoran, Quaker Oats, ASARCO, United, Delta, Northwest, ITT, International Harvester, Xerox, Boeing, Westinghouse, Hewlett-Packard, Honeywell, International Paper, Pfizer, Motorola, Monsanto, Union Carbide and General Foods.

The Rockefeller Foundation has close financial ties to both Ford and Carnegie Foundations. Other family philanthropic endeavors include Rockefeller Brothers Fund, Rockefeller Institute for Medical Research, General Education Board, Rockefeller University and the University of Chicago, which churns out a steady stream of far right economists as apologists for international capital, including Milton Friedman.

The family owns 30 Rockefeller Plaza, where the national Christmas tree is lighted every year, and Rockefeller Center. David Rockefeller was instrumental in the construction of the World Trade Center towers. The main Rockefeller family home is a hulking complex in upstate New York known as Pocantico Hills. They also own a 32-room 5th Avenue duplex in Manhattan, a mansion in Washington, DC, Monte Sacro Ranch in Venezuela, coffee plantations in Ecuador, several farms in Brazil, an estate at Seal Harbor, Maine and resorts in the Caribbean, Hawaii and Puerto Rico. [20]

The Dulles and Rockefeller families are cousins. Allen Dulles created the CIA, assisted the Nazis, covered up the Kennedy hit from his Warren Commission perch and struck a deal with the Muslim Brotherhood to create mind-controlled assassins. Brother John Foster Dulles presided over the phony Goldman Sachs trusts before the 1929 stock market crash and helped his brother overthrow governments in Iran and Guatemala. Both were Skull & Bones, CFR members and 33rd Degree Masons.

The Rockefellers were instrumental in forming the depopulation-oriented Club of Rome at their family estate in Bellagio, Italy. Their Pocantico Hills estate gave birth to the Trilateral Commission. The family is a major funder of the eugenics movement which spawned Hitler, human cloning and the current DNA obsession in US scientific circles.

John Rockefeller Jr. headed the Population Council until his death. [21] His namesake son is a Senator from West Virginia. Brother Winthrop Rockefeller was Lieutenant Governor of Arkansas and is the most powerful man in that state. In an October 1975 interview with *Playboy* magazine, Vice-President Nelson Rockefeller - who was also Governor of New York - articulated his family's patronizing worldview, "I am a great believer in planning - economic, social, political, military, total world planning."

But of all the Rockefeller brothers, it is Trilateral Commission (TC) founder and Chase Manhattan Chairman David who has spearheaded the family's fascist agenda on a global scale. He defended the Shah of Iran, the South African apartheid regime and the Chilean Pinochet *junta*. He was the biggest financier of the CFR, the TC and (during the Vietnam War) the Committee for an Effective and Durable Peace in Asia - a contract bonanza for those who made their living off the conflict.

Nixon asked him to be Secretary of Treasury, but Rockefeller declined the job, knowing his power was much greater at the helm of the Chase. According to writer Gary Allen, in 1973, "David Rockefeller met with twenty-seven heads of state, including the rulers of Russia and Red China." Following the 1975 Nugan Hand/CIA *coup* against Australian Prime Minister Gough Whitlam, British Crown-appointed successor Malcolm Fraser sped to the US, where he met with President Gerald Ford only *after* conferring with David Rockefeller. [22]

Freemasonry and the Bank of the United States

In 1789 Alexander Hamilton became the first Treasury Secretary of the United States. Hamilton was one of many founding fathers who were Freemasons. He had close relations with the Rothschild family which owns the Bank of England and leads the European Freemason movement. George Washington, Benjamin Franklin, John Jay, Ethan Allen, Samuel Adams, Patrick Henry, John Brown and Roger Sherman were all Masons.

Roger Livingston helped Sherman and Franklin write the Declaration of Independence. He gave George Washington his oaths of office while he was Grand Master of the New York Grand Lodge of Freemasons. Washington himself was Grand Master of the Virginia Lodge. Of the General Officers in the Revolutionary Army, thirty-three were Masons. [23] This was highly symbolic since 33rd Degree Masons are said to be Illuminated.

Populist founding fathers led by John Adams, Thomas Jefferson, James Madison and Thomas Paine - none of whom were Masons - wanted to completely severe ties with the British Crown, but were overruled by the Masonic faction led by Washington, Hamilton and Grand Master of the St. Andrews Lodge in Boston General Joseph Warren, who wanted to "defy Parliament but remain loyal to the Crown". [24] St. Andrews Lodge was the hub of New World Masonry and began issuing Knights Templar Degrees in 1769. All US Masonic lodges are to this day warranted by the British Crown.

The First Continental Congress convened in Philadelphia in 1774 under the Presidency of Peyton Randolph, who succeeded Washington as Grand Master of the Virginia Lodge. The Second Continental Congress convened in 1775 under the Presidency of Freemason John Hancock. Peyton's brother William succeeded him as Virginia Lodge Grand Master and became the leading proponent of centralization and federalism at the First Constitutional Convention in 1787. The federalism at the heart of the US Constitution is identical to the federalism laid out in the Freemason's *Anderson's Constitutions of 1723*.

William Randolph became the nation's first Attorney General and Secretary of State under George Washington, while his family returned to England loyal to the Crown. John Marshall, the nation's first Supreme Court Justice, was also a Mason. [25]

When Benjamin Franklin journeyed to France to seek financial help for American revolutionaries, his meetings took place at Rothschild banks. He brokered arms sales *via* German Mason Baron von Steuben. His Committees of Correspondence operated through Freemason channels and paralleled a British spy network. In 1776 Franklin became *de facto* Ambassador to France. In 1779 he became Grand Master of the French *Neuf Soeurs* (Nine Sisters) Lodge, to which John Paul Jones and Voltaire belonged. Franklin was also a member of the more secretive Royal Lodge of Commanders of the Temple West of Carcasonne, whose members included Frederick Prince of Whales.

While Franklin preached temperance in the US, he cavorted wildly with his Lodge brothers in Europe. Franklin served as Postmaster General from the 1750's to 1775 - a role traditionally relegated to British spies. [26]

With Rothschild financing Alexander Hamilton founded two New York banks, including Bank of New York. [27] He died in a gun battle with Aaron Burr, who founded Bank of Manhattan with Kuhn Loeb financing. Hamilton exemplified the contempt which the Eight Families hold towards common people, once stating, "All communities divide themselves into the few and the many. The first are the rich and the well born, the others the mass of the people...The people are turbulent and changing; they seldom judge and determine right. Give therefore to the first class a distinct, permanent share of government. They will check the unsteadiness of the second."[28]

Hamilton was only the first in a series of Eight Families' cronies to hold the key position of Treasury Secretary. In recent times Kennedy Treasury Secretary Douglas Dillon came from Dillon Read, Nixon Treasury Secretaries David Kennedy and William Simon came from Continental Illinois Bank and Salomon Brothers respectively, Carter Treasury Secretary Michael Blumenthal came from Goldman Sachs, Reagan Treasury Secretary Donald Regan came from Merrill Lynch, Bush Sr. Treasury Secretary Nicholas Brady came from Dillon Read and both Clinton Treasury Secretary Robert Rubin and Bush Jr. Treasury Secretary Henry Paulson came from Goldman Sachs.

Thomas Jefferson argued that the United States needed a publicly-owned central bank so that European monarchs and aristocrats could not use the printing of money to control the affairs of the new nation. Jefferson extolled, "A country which expects to remain ignorant and free...expects that which has never been and that which will never be. There is scarcely a King in a hundred who would not, if he could, follow the example of Pharaoh – get first all the people's money, then all their lands and then make them and their children servants forever...banking establishments are more dangerous than standing armies. Already they have raised up a money aristocracy."[29]

Jefferson watched as the Euro-banking conspiracy to control the United States unfolded, weighing in, "Single acts of tyranny may be ascribed to the accidental opinion of the day, but a series of oppressions begun at a distinguished period, unalterable through every change of ministers, too plainly prove a deliberate, systematic plan of reducing us to slavery".

But the Rothschild-sponsored Hamilton's arguments for a private US central bank carried the day. In 1791 the Bank of the United States was founded, with the Rothschilds as main owners. The bank's charter was to run out in 1811. Public opinion ran in favor of revoking the charter and replacing it with a Jeffersonian public central bank. The debate was postponed as the nation was plunged by the Euro-bankers into the War of 1812. Amidst a climate of fear and economic hardship, Hamilton's bank got its charter renewed in 1816.

Old Hickory and Honest Abe

In 1828 Andrew Jackson took a run at the US Presidency. Throughout his campaign he railed against the international bankers who controlled the Bank of the United States (BUS). Jackson ranted, "You are a den of vipers. I intend to expose you and by Eternal God I will rout you out. If the people understood the rank injustices of our money and banking system there would be a revolution before morning."

Jackson won the election and revoked the bank's charter stating, "The Act seems to be predicated on an erroneous idea that the present shareholders have a prescriptive right to not only the favor, but the bounty of the government...for their benefit does this Act exclude the whole American people from competition in the purchase of this monopoly. Present stockholders and those inheriting their rights as successors be established a privileged order, clothed both with great political power and enjoying immense pecuniary advantages from their connection with government. Should its influence be concentrated under the operation of such an Act as this, in the hands of a self-elected directory whose interests are identified with those of the foreign stockholders, will there not be cause to tremble for the independence of our country in war...controlling our currency, receiving our public monies and holding thousands of our citizens independence, it would be more formidable and dangerous than the naval and military power of the enemy. It is to be regretted that the rich and powerful too often bend the acts of government for selfish purposes...to make the rich richer and more powerful. Many of our rich men have not been content with equal protection and equal benefits, but have besought us to make them richer by acts of Congress. I have done my duty to this country."[30]

Populism prevailed and Jackson was re-elected. In 1835 he was the target of the first assassination attempt on a US President. The gunman was Richard Lawrence, who confessed that he was, "in touch with the powers in Europe". [31] Still, in 1836 Jackson refused to renew the BUS charter. Under his watch the US national debt went to zero for the first and last time in our nation's history. This angered the international bankers whose primary income is derived from interest payments on debt. BUS President Nicholas Biddle cut off funding to the US government in 1842, plunging the US into a depression. Biddle was an agent for the Paris-based Jacob Rothschild. [32]

The Mexican War was simultaneously sprung on Jackson. A few years later the Civil War was unleashed, with London bankers backing the Union and French bankers backing the South. The Lehman family made a fortune smuggling arms to the south and cotton to the north. By 1861 the US was $100 million in debt. New

President Abraham Lincoln snubbed the Euro-bankers again, issuing Lincoln Greenbacks to pay Union Army bills. The *Times of London* now called for the "destruction of the US government".

The Euro-banker-written *Hazard Circular* was exposed and circulated throughout the country by angry populists. It stated, "The European Bankers favor the end of slavery...the European plan is that capital money lenders shall control labor by controlling wages. The great debt that capitalists will see is made out of the war and must be used to control the valve of money. To accomplish this government bonds must be used as a banking basis. We are now awaiting Secretary of Treasury Salmon Chase to make that recommendation. It will not allow Greenbacks to circulate as money as we cannot control that. We control bonds and through them banking issues".

The 1863 National Banking Act reinstated a private US central bank and Chase's war bonds were issued. Lincoln was re-elected the next year, vowing to repeal the act after he took his January 1865 oaths of office. Before he could act, he was assassinated at the Ford Theatre by John Wilkes Booth. Booth had major connections to the international bankers. His granddaughter wrote *This One Mad Act*, which details Booth's contact with "mysterious Europeans" just before the Lincoln assassination.

Following the Lincoln hit, Booth was whisked away by members of a secret society known as Knights of the Golden Circle (KGC). KGC had close ties to the French Society of Seasons, which produced Karl Marx. KGC had fomented much of the tension that caused the Civil War and President Lincoln had specifically targeted the group. Booth was a KGC member and was connected through Confederate Secretary of State Judah Benjamin to the House of Rothschild. Benjamin fled to England after the war. [33]

Nearly a century after Lincoln was assassinated for issuing Greenbacks, President Kennedy was assassinated for issuing silver-backed United States Notes. The US sank further into debt. Its citizens were terrorized into silence. If they could kill the President they could kill anyone.

The House of Rothschild

The Rothschild family combined with the Dutch House of Orange to found Bank of Amsterdam in the early 1600's as the world's first central bank. Prince William of Orange married into the English House of Windsor, taking King James II's daughter Mary as his bride. The Orange Order Brotherhood, which has recently fomented Northern Ireland Protestant violence, put William III on the English throne where he ruled both Holland and Britain. In 1694 William III teamed up with the Rothschilds to launch the Bank of England.

The Old Lady of Threadneedle Street - as the Bank of England is known - is surrounded by thirty foot walls. Three floors beneath it the third largest stock of gold bullion in the world is stored. [34] The daily London gold "fixing" occurs at the N. M. Rothschild Bank. As Bank of England Deputy Governor George Blunden put it, "Fear is what makes the bank's powers so acceptable. The bank is able to exert its influence when people are dependent on us and fear losing their privileges or when they are frightened."[35]

Mayer Amschel Rothschild sold the British government German Hessian mercenaries to fight against American Revolutionaries, diverting the proceeds to his brother Nathan in London, where N.M. (Nathan and Mayer) Rothschild & Sons was established. Mayer was a serious student of Cabala and launched his fortune on money embezzled from William IX - royal administrator of the Hesse-Kassel region and a prominent Freemason.

Rothschild-controlled Barings bankrolled the Chinese opium and African slave trades. It financed the Louisiana Purchase. When several states defaulted on its loans, Barings bribed Daniel Webster to make speeches stressing the virtues of loan repayment. The states held their ground, so the House of Rothschild cut off the money spigot in 1842, plunging the US into a deep depression. It was often said that the wealth of the Rothschilds depended on the bankruptcy of nations. Mayer Amschel Rothschild once said, "I care not who controls a nation's political affairs, so long as I control her currency".

War didn't hurt the family fortune either. The House of Rothschild financed the Prussian War, the Crimean War and the

British attempt to seize the Suez Canal from the French. Nathan Rothschild made a huge financial bet on Napoleon at the Battle of Waterloo, while also funding the Duke of Wellington's peninsular campaign *against* Napoleon. Both the Mexican War and the Civil War were goldmines for the family.

A Rothschild family biography mentions a London meeting where an "International Banking Syndicate" decided to pit the American North against the South as part of a "divide and conquer" strategy. German Chancellor Otto von Bismarck once stated, "The division of the United States into federations of equal force was decided long before the Civil War. These bankers were afraid that the United States...would upset their financial domination over the world. The voice of the Rothschilds prevailed."

Rothschild biographer Derek Wilson says the family was the official European banker to the US government and strong supporters of the Bank of the United States. [36] Family biographer Niall Ferguson notes a "substantial and unexplained gap" in private Rothschild correspondence between 1854-1860. He says all copies of outgoing letters written by the London Rothschilds during this Civil War period "were destroyed at the orders of successive partners". [37]

French and British troops had, at the height of the Civil War, encircled the US. The British sent 11,000 troops to Crown-controlled Canada, which gave safe harbor to Confederate agents. France's Napoleon III installed Austrian Hapsburg family member Archduke Maximilian as his puppet emperor in Mexico, where French troops massed on the Texas border. Only an 11th-hour deployment of two Russian warship fleets by US ally Czar Alexander II in 1863 saved the United States from re-colonization. [38] That same year the *Chicago Tribune* blasted, "Belmont (August Belmont was a US Rothschild agent and had a Triple Crown horse race named in his honor) and the Rothschilds...who have been buying up Confederate war bonds."

Salmon Rothschild said of a deceased President Lincoln, "He rejects all forms of compromise. He has the appearance of a peasant and can only tell barroom stories." Baron Jacob Rothschild was equally flattering towards the US citizenry. He once commented to US Minister to Belgium Henry Sanford on the over half a million

Americans who died during the Civil War, "When your patient is desperately sick, you try desperate measures, even to bloodletting." Salmon and Jacob were merely carrying forth a family tradition. A few generations earlier Mayer Amschel Rothschild bragged of his investment strategy, "When the streets of Paris are running in blood, I buy".

Mayer Rothschild's sons were known as the Frankfurt Five. The eldest - Amschel - ran the family's Frankfurt bank with his father, while Nathan ran London operations. Youngest son Jacob set up shop in Paris, while Salomon ran the Vienna branch and Karl was off to Naples. Author Frederick Morton estimates that by 1850 the Rothschilds were worth over $10 billion. [39] Some researchers believe that their fortune today exceeds $100 trillion.

The Warburgs, Kuhn Loebs, Goldman Sachs, Schiffs and Rothschilds have intermarried into one big happy banking family. The Warburg family - which controls Deutsche Bank and *Banque Paribas* - tied up with the Rothschilds in 1814 in Hamburg, while Kuhn Loeb powerhouse Jacob Schiff shared quarters with Rothschilds in 1785. Schiff immigrated to America in 1865. He joined forces with Abraham Kuhn and married Solomon Loeb's daughter. Loeb and Kuhn married each others sisters and the Kuhn Loeb dynasty was consummated. Felix Warburg married Jacob Schiff's daughter. Two Goldman daughters married two sons of the Sachs family, creating Goldman Sachs. In 1806 Nathan Rothschild married the oldest daughter of Levi Barent Cohen, a leading financier in London. [40] Merrill Lynch super bull Abby Joseph Cohen and Clinton Secretary of Defense William Cohen are thus descended from Rothschilds.

Today the Rothschild's control a far-flung financial empire, which includes majority stakes in most world central banks. The Edmond de Rothschild clan owns the *Banque Privee SA* in Lugano, Switzerland and the Rothschild Bank AG of Zurich. The family of Jacob Lord Rothschild owns the powerful *Rothschild Italia* in Milan. They are members of the exclusive Club of the Isles, which provides capital for George Soros' Quantum Fund NV, which made a killing in 1998-1999 destroying the currencies of Thailand, Indonesia and Russia. Soros was a major shareholder at Harken Energy.

Quantum NV handles $11-14 billion in assets and operates from the Dutch island of Curacao, in the shadow of massive Royal Dutch/Shell and Exxon Mobil refineries. Curacao was recently cited by an OECD Task Force on Money Laundering as a major drug money laundering nation. The Club of Isles group which funds Quantum is led by the Rothschilds and includes Queen Elizabeth II and other wealthy European aristocrats and Black Nobility. Fugitive Swiss financier and Mossad cutout Marc Rich, whose business interests were recently taken over by the Russian mafia Alfa Group, is also part of the Soros network. [41]

Ties to drug money are nothing new to the Rothschilds. N. M. Rothschild & Sons was at the epicenter of the BCCI scandal, but escaped the limelight when a warehouse full of documents conveniently burned to the ground around the time Rothschild-controlled Bank of England shut BCCI down. Perhaps the largest repository for Rothschild wealth today is Rothschilds Continuation Holdings AG - a secretive Swiss-based bank holding company. By the late 1990s scions of the Rothschild global empire were Barons Guy and Elie de Rothschild in France and Lord Jacob and Sir Evelyn Rothschild in Britain. [42] Evelyn is chairman of the *Economist*.

Knights of the Roundtable

The Rothschilds exert political control through the secretive Business Roundtable, which they created in 1909 with the help of Lord Alfred Milner and South African industrialist Cecil Rhodes-whose Rhodes Scholarship is granted by Cambridge University, out of which oil industry propagandist Cambridge Energy Research Associates operates. Rhodes founded De Beers and Standard Chartered Bank. Milner financed the Russian Bolsheviks on Rothschild's behalf, with help from Jacob Schiff and Max Warburg.

In 1917 British Foreign Secretary Arthur Balfour penned a letter to Zionist Second Lord Lionel Walter Rothschild in which he expressed support for a Jewish homeland on Palestinian-controlled lands in the Middle East. [43] The Balfour Declaration justified the brutal seizure of Palestinian lands for the post-WWII establishment of Israel. Israel would serve, not as some high-minded "Jewish homeland", but as lynchpin in Rothschild/Eight Families control over the world's oil supply. Baron Edmond de Rothschild built the first oil pipeline from the Red Sea to the Mediterranean to bring BP Iranian oil to Israel. He founded Israeli General Bank and Paz Oil. He is considered by many the father of modern Israel. [44]

Roundtable inner Circle of Initiates included Lord Milner, Cecil Rhodes, Arthur Balfour, Albert Grey and Lord Nathan Rothschild. The Roundtable takes its name from the legendary knight of King Arthur, whose tale of the Holy Grail is paramount to the *Illuminati* notion of *Sangreal* or holy blood. According to former British Intelligence officer John Coleman, who wrote *Committee of 300*, "Round Tablers armed with immense wealth from gold, diamond and drug monopolies fanned out throughout the world to take control of fiscal and monetary policies and political leadership in all countries where they operated."

While Cecil Rhodes and the Oppenheimers went to South Africa, the Kuhn Loebs were off to re-colonize America. Rudyard Kipling was sent to India, the Schiffs and Warburgs manhandled Russia, while the Rothschilds, Lazards and Israel Moses Seifs pushed into the MidEast. In Princeton, New Jersey the Round Table founded the Institute for Advanced Study (IAS) as partner to its All Souls College at Oxford. IAS was funded by the Rockefeller's General Education Board. IAS members Robert Oppenheimer, Neils Bohr and Albert Einstein created the atomic bomb. [45]

In 1919 Rothschild's Business Roundtable spawned the Royal Institute of International Affairs (RIIA) in London. The RIIA soon sponsored sister organizations around the globe, including the US Council on Foreign Relations (CFR), the Asian Institute of Pacific Relations, the Canadian Institute of International Affairs, the Brussels-based *Institute des Relations Internationales*, the Danish Foreign Policy Society, the Indian Council of World Affairs and the Australian Institute of International Affairs. [854] Other affiliates popped up in France, Turkey, Italy, Yugoslavia and Greece.

The RIIA is a registered charity of the Queen and, according to its annual reports, is funded largely by the Four Horsemen. Former British Foreign Secretary and Kissinger Associates co-founder Lord Carrington is President of both the RIIA and the Bilderbergers. [46] The inner circle at RIIA is dominated by Knights of St. John

Jerusalem, Knights of Malta, Knights Templar and 33rd Degree Scottish Rite Freemasons. The Knights of St. John were founded in 1070 and answer directly to the British House of Windsor. Their leading bloodline is the Villiers dynasty, which the Hong Kong Matheson family married into. The Lytton family also married into the Villiers gang.

Colonel Edward Bulwer-Lytton led the English *Rosicrucian* secret society, which Shakespeare opaquely referred to as Rosencranz, while the Freemasons took the role of Guildenstern. Lytton was spiritual father of both the RIIA and Nazi fascism. In 1871 he penned a novel titled, *Vril: The Power of the Coming Race.* Seventy years later the Vril Society received ample mention in Adolf Hitler's *Mein Kampf.* Lytton's son became Viceroy to India in 1876 just before opium production spiked in that country. Lytton's good friend Rudyard Kipling introduced the *swastika* to India and later worked under Lord Beaverbrook as Propaganda Minister, alongside Sir Charles Hambro of the Hambros banking dynasty.

James Bruce, ancestor to Scottish Rite Freemason founder Sir Robert the Bruce, was the 8th Earl of Elgin. He supervised the Caribbean slave trade as Jamaican Governor General from 1842-1846. He was Britain's Ambassador to China during the Second Opium War. His brother Frederick was Colonial Secretary of Hong Kong during both Opium Wars. Both were prominent Freemasons. British Lord Palmerston, who ran the Opium Wars, was a blood relative of the Bruce monarchy, as was his Foreign Secretary John Russell, grandfather of Bertrand Russell. [47]

Children of the Roundtable elite are members of a Dionysian cult known as Children of the Sun. Initiates include Aldous Huxley, T. S. Eliot, D. H. Lawrence and H. G. Wells. Wells headed British intelligence during WWI. His books speak of a "one-world brain" and "a police of the mind". William Butler Yeats, another Sun member, was a pal of Aleister Crowley. The two formed an Isis Cult based on a Madam Blavatsky manuscript, which called on the British aristocracy to organize itself into an Isis Aryan priesthood. [48] Most prominent writers of English literature came from the ranks of the Roundtable. All promoted Empire expansion, however subtly. Blavatsky's Theosophical Society and Bulwer-Lytton's

Rosicrucians joined forces to form the Thule Society out of which the Nazis emerged.

Aleister Crowley formed the British parallel to the Thule Society, the Isis-Urania Hermetic Order of the Golden Dawn. He tutored LSD guru Aldus Huxley, who arrived in the US in 1952, the same year the CIA launched its MK-ULTRA mind control program with help from the Warburg-owned Swiss Sandoz Laboratories and Rockefeller cousin Allen Dulles - OSS Station Chief in Berne. Dulles may have received information from the Muslim Brotherhood Saudi monarchy regarding the creation of mind-controlled Assassins. Dulles' assistant was James Warburg.

The Atlantic Union (AU) was an RIIA affiliate founded by Cecil Rhodes - who dreamed of returning the US to the British Crown. In 1939 AU set up its first offices in America in space donated by Nelson Rockefeller at 10 E 40th St in New York City. Every year from 1949-1976 an AU resolution was floored in Congress calling for a repeal of the Declaration of Independence and a "new world order".

Another RIIA affiliate was United World Federalists (UWF) - founded by Norman Cousins and Dulles assistant James P. Warburg. UWF's motto was "One world or none". Its first president Cord Meyer stepped down to take a key position in Allen Dulles' CIA. Meyer articulated UWF's goal, "Once having joined the One-World Federated Government, no nation could secede or revolt...with the atom bomb in its possession the Federal Government would blow that nation off the face of the earth."

In 1950 UWF founder and Dulles' assistant James Warburg, whose elders Max and Paul sat on the board of Nazi business combine IG Farben, testified before the Senate Foreign Relations Committee, "We shall have world government whether or not you like it - by conquest or consent." The AU and UAF are close to the CFR and the Trilateral Commission (TC) - founded by David Rockefeller and Zbigniew Brzezinski in 1974.

The TC published *The Triangle Papers* which extended the "special relationship between the US and Western Europe" to include Japan, which was fast becoming creditor to the rest of the world. Former Federal Reserve Chairman Paul Volcker was TC Chairman. TC/CFR insider Harvard Professor Samuel Huntington, who most recently has argued for a "Clash of Civilizations" between the West and the Muslim world, wrote in the TC publication *Crisis in Democracy*, "...a government which lacks authority will have little ability short of cataclysmic crisis to impose on its people the sacrifices which may be necessary."

The *Illuminati*

The *Illuminati* serves as ruling council to all secret societies. They encouraged US independence from Britain so that American affairs could be secretly run by the Crown without interference from British Parliament. Its roots go back to the Guardians of Light in Atlantis, the Brotherhood of the Snake in Sumeria, the Afghan *Roshaniya*, the Egyptian Mystery Schools and the Genoese families who bankrolled the Roman Empire and hung Jesus Christ on the cross for exposing them. British Prime Minister Benjamin Disraeli, who "handled" mafia-founder and 33rd Degree Mason Guiseppe Mazzini, alluded to the *Illuminati* in a speech before the House of Commons in 1856 warning, "There is in Italy a power which we seldom mention. I mean the secret societies. Europe...is covered with a network of secret societies just as the surfaces of the earth are covered with a network of railroads."[49]

The *Illuminati* is to these secret societies what the Bank of International Settlements is to the Eight Families central bankers. And their constituencies are exactly the same. The forerunners of the Freemasons - the Knights Templar - founded the concept of banking and created a "bond market" as a means to control European nobles through war debts. The Templars claim to possess secret knowledge that Jesus Christ married Mary Magdalene, fathered children and was the son of Joseph of Arimathea.

Joseph was the son of King Solomon. Solomon's Temple is the model for Masonic Temples, which occur without fail in every town of any size in America. It was a place of ill repute where fornicating, drunkenness and human sacrifice were the norm. It's location on Jerusalem's Mount Moriah may have been an Anunnaki flight control center. The Crusader Knights Templar looted a huge store of gold and numerous sacred artifacts from beneath the

Temple. King Solomon was the son of King David - who during his 1015 BC reign massacred thousands of people. This claimed lineage to the House of David is what the *Illuminati* use to justify their global control.

Author David Icke calls King David "a butcher" and asserts that the king wrote a good chunk of the Bible. His son Solomon killed his own brother to become King. He advised Egyptian Pharaoh Shiskak I, marrying his daughter. Solomon studied at Akhenaton's Egyptian Mystery Schools, where mind control was rampant. The Grand Lodge of Cairo spawned both the Assassins and the terrorist Afghan *Roshaniya*. Solomon returned to Jerusalem to build his Temple with help from Egyptian Brotherhood brick Freemasons.

The Canaanite Brotherhood was headed by the god/king Melchizedek, who may have been an Annunaki. The King focused on a Hebrew understanding of the Ancient Mysteries. The Order of Melchizedek became the secret society associated with the Cabala. King Solomon developed his vast wisdom studying the Sumerian Tables of Destiny which Abraham had possessed. Abraham may have also been of Anunnaki origin.

Both he and Melchizedek had been tutored by the Sumerian Brotherhood of the Snake, whose name may have something to do with the Biblical creation story, where Adam and Eve are tempted from a bountiful garden of Eden (a hunting and gathering existence?) into a world of "sin and servitude" by a snake. When the Bible says that the first couple ate the forbidden fruit, could it mean that Eve was impregnated by the snake - an Annunaki serpent - thus damning all Adamus to a life of toil under serpent king bloodline control?

The basis of the Sumerian Tables of Destiny which Abraham possessed became known as *Ha Qabala*, Hebrew for "light and knowledge". Those who understood these cryptic secrets, said to be encoded throughout the Old Testament, are referred to deferentially as Ram. The phrase is used in Celtic, Buddhist and Hindu spiritual circles as well. The Knights Templar brought Cabbalistic knowledge to Europe when they returned from their Middle East Crusade adventures. [50]

The Knights created the *Prieure de Sion* on Mt. Zion near Jerusalem in the 11th century to guard such holy relics as the Shroud of Turin, the Ark of the Covenant and the Hapsburg family's Spear of Destiny - which was used to kill Jesus Christ. The Priory's more important purpose was to guard Templar gold and to preserve the bloodline of Jesus – the royal *Sangreal* – which they believe is carried forth by the French Bourbon Merovingan family and the related Hapsburg monarchs of Spain and Austria. [51] The French Lorraine dynasty, which descended from the Merovingans, married into the House of Hapsburg to acquire the throne of Austria.

The Hapsburgs ran the Holy Roman Empire until its dissolution in 1806, through King Charles V and others. The family traces its roots back to a Swiss estate known as Habichtburg, which was built in 1020. The Hapsburgs are an integral part of the Priory of Sion. Many researchers are convinced that Spain's Hapsburg King Philip will be crowned *Sangreal* World King in Jerusalem. The Hapsburgs are related to the Rothschilds through Holy Roman Emperor Frederick Barbarossa's second son Archibald II.

The Rothschilds - leaders in Cabala, Freemasonry and the Knights Templar - sit at the apex of the both the *Illuminati* and the Eight Families banking cartel. The family accumulated its vast wealth issuing war bonds to Black Nobility for centuries, including the British Windsors, the French Bourbons, the German von Thurn und Taxis, the Italian Savoys and the Austrian and Spanish Hapsburgs.

Author David Icke believes the Rothschilds represent the head of the Anunnaki Serpent Kings, stating, "They (Rothschilds) had the crown heads of Europe in debt to them and this included the Black Nobility dynasty, the Hapsburgs, who ruled the Holy Roman Empire for 600 years. The Rothschilds also control the Bank of England. If there was a war, the Rothschilds were behind the scenes, creating conflict and funding both sides."[52]

The Rothschilds and the Warburgs are main stockholders of the German *Bundesbank*. [53] Rothschilds control Japan's biggest banking house Nomura Securities *via* a tie-up between Edmund Rothschild and Tsunao Okumura. The Rothschilds are the richest and most powerful family in the world. They are also inbred. Over half of the last generation of Rothschild progeny married within the family, presumably to preserve their *Sangreal*.

The 1782 Great Seal of the United States is loaded with *Illuminati* symbolism. So is the reverse side of the US $1 Federal

Reserve Note, which was designed by Freemasons. The pyramid on the left side represents those in Egypt - possibly space beacon/energy source to the Anunnaki - whose Pharaohs oversaw the building of the pyramids using Israelite slave labor.

The pyramid is an important symbol for the *Illuminati* bankers. They employ Triads, Trilaterals and Trinities to create a society ruled by an elite *Sangreal* few presiding over the masses - as represented by a pyramid. The Brotherhood of the Snake worshiped a Trinity of Isis, Osirus and Horus - who may have been Anunnaki offspring. The Brotherhood spread the concept of Trinity to Christian (Father, Son and Holy Spirit), Hindu (Brahma, Shiva and Krishna) and Buddhist (Buddha, Dharma and Sangha) faiths. [54]

The eye atop the pyramid depicted on the $1 bill is the all-seeing eye of the Afghan *Roshaniya*, known alternately as The Order and Order of the Quest - names adopted by Skull & Bones, *Germanorden* and the JASON Society. [55] *Novus Ordo Seclorum* appears beneath the pyramid, while *Annuit Coeptis* appears above the all-seeing eye. *Annuit Coeptis* means "may he smile upon our endeavors (Great Work of Ages)". Above the eagle on the right side of the note are the words *E Pluribus Unum*, Latin for "out of many one". The eagle clutches 13 arrows and 13 olive branches, while 13 stars appear above the eagle's head. America was founded with 13 colonies. Templar pirate Jaques deMolay was executed on Friday the 13th.

The numbers 3, 9, 13 and 33 are significant to the secret societies. The Bilderberger Group has a powerful Policy Committee of 13 members. It is one of 3 committees of 13 which answer to Prince Bernhard - member of the Hapsburg family and leader of the Black Nobility. The Bilderberg Policy Committee answers to a Rothschild Round Table of 9. [56]

The Federal Reserve

United World Federalists founder James Warburg's father was Paul Warburg, who financed Hitler with help from Brown Brothers Harriman partner Prescott Bush. [57] Colonel Ely Garrison was a close friend of both President Teddy Roosevelt and President

Woodrow Wilson. Garrison wrote in *Roosevelt, Wilson and the Federal Reserve*, "Paul Warburg was the man who got the Federal Reserve Act together after the Aldrich Plan aroused such nationwide resentment and opposition. The mastermind of both plans was Baron Alfred Rothschild of London."

The Aldrich Plan was hatched at a secret 1910 meeting at JP Morgan's private resort on Jekyl Island, SC between Rockefeller lieutenant Nelson Aldrich and Paul Warburg of the German Warburg banking dynasty. Aldrich, a New York congressman, later married into the Rockefeller family. His son Winthrop Aldrich chaired Chase Manhattan Bank. While the bankers met, Colonel Edward House, another Rockefeller stooge and close confidant of President Woodrow Wilson, was busy convincing Wilson of the importance of a private central bank and the introduction of a national income tax. A member of House's staff was General Julius Klein, the British MI6 Permindex insider.

Wilson didn't need much convincing, since he was beholden to copper magnate Cleveland Dodge, whose namesake Phelps Dodge is one of the biggest mining companies in the world. Dodge bankrolled Wilson's political career. Wilson wrote his inaugural speech on Dodge's yacht. [58] Wilson was a classmate of both Dodge and Cyrus McCormick at Princeton. Both were directors at Rockefeller's National City Bank (now Citigroup). Wilson's main focus was on overcoming public distrust of the bankers, which New York City Mayor John Hylan echoed in 1911 when he argued, "The real menace to our republic is the invisible government which, like a giant octopus, sprawls its slimy length over our city, state and nation. At the head is a small group of banking houses, generally referred to as the international bankers". [59]

But the Eight Families prevailed. In 1913 the Federal Reserve Bank was born, with Paul Warburg its first Governor. Four years later the US entered World War I, after a secret society known as the Black Hand assassinated Archduke Ferdinand and his Hapsburg wife. The Archduke's friend Count Czerin later said, "A year before the war he informed me that the Masons had resolved upon his death."[60] That same year, Bolsheviks overthrew the Hohehzollern monarchy in Russia with help from Max Warburg and Jacob Schiff, while the Balfour Declaration leading to the creation of Israel was penned to Zionist Second Lord Rothschild.

In the 1920's Baron Edmund de Rothschild founded the Palestine Economics Commission, while Kuhn Loeb's Manhattan offices helped Rothschild form a network to smuggle weapons to Zionist death squads bent on seizing Palestinian lands. General Julius Klein oversaw the operation and headed the US Army Counterintelligence Corps, which later produced Henry Kissinger. Klein diverted Marshall Plan aid to Europe to Zionist terror cells in Palestine after WWII, channeling the funds through the Sonneborn Institute, which was controlled by Baltimore chemical magnate Rudolph Sonneborn. His wife Dorothy Schiff is related to the Warburgs. [61]

The Kuhn Loebs came to Manhattan with the Warburgs. At the same time the Bronfmans came to Canada as part of the Moses Montefiore Jewish Colonization Committee. The Montefiores have carried out the dirty work of Genoese nobility since the 13th Century. The di Spadaforas served that function for the Italian House of Savoy, which was bankrolled by the Israel Moses Seif family for which Israel is named. Lord Harold Sebag Montefiore is current head of the Jerusalem Foundation, the Zionist wing of the Knights of St. John's Jerusalem. The "liquorman" Bronfmans tied up with Arnold Rothstein, a product of the Rothschild's dry goods empire, to found organized crime in New York City. Rothstein was succeeded by Lucky Luciano, Meyer Lansky, Robert Vesco and Santos Trafficante. The Bronfmans are intermarried with the Rothschilds, Loebs and Lamberts. [62]

The year 1917 also saw the 16th Amendment added to the US Constitution, levying a national income tax, though it was ratified by only two of the required 36 states. The IRS is a private corporation registered in Delaware. [63] Four years earlier the Rockefeller Foundation was launched, to shield family wealth from the new income tax provisions, while steering public opinion through social engineering. One of its tentacles was the General Education Board.

In Occasional Letter #1 the Board states, "In our dreams we have limitless resources and the people yield themselves with perfect docility to our molding hands. The present education conventions fade from their minds and, unhampered by tradition, we will work our own good will upon a grateful and responsive rural folk. We shall try not to make these people or any of their children into philosophers or men of learning or men of science...of whom we have ample supply."[64]

Though most Americans think of the Federal Reserve as a government institution, it is privately held by the Eight Families. The Secret Service is employed, not by the Executive Branch, but by the Federal Reserve. [65]

An exchange between Sen. Edward Kennedy (D-MA) and Fed Chairman Paul Volcker at Senate hearings in 1982 is instructive. Kennedy must have thought of his older brother John when he told Volcker that if he were before the committee as a member of US Treasury things would be much different. Volcker, puffing on a cigar, responded cavalierly, "That's probably true. But I believe it was intentionally designed this way". [66] Rep. Lee Hamilton (D-IN) put it to Volcker that, "People realize that what that board of yours does has a very profound impact on their pocketbooks, and yet it is a group of people basically inaccessible to them and unaccountable to them."

President Wilson spoke of, "a power so organized, so complete, so pervasive, that they had better not speak above their breaths when they speak in condemnation of it." Rep. Charles Lindberg (D-NY) was more blunt, railing against Wilson's Federal Reserve Act, which had cleverly been dubbed the "People's Bill". Lindberg declared that the Act would, "...establish the most gigantic trust on earth...When the president signs this act, the invisible government by the money power will be legitimized. The law will create inflation whenever the trusts want inflation. From now on, depressions will be scientifically created. The invisible government by the money power, proven to exist by the Money Trust Investigation, will be legalized. The whole central bank concept was engineered by the very group it was supposed to strip of power". [67]

The Fed is made up of all banks in the US, but the New York Federal Reserve Bank controls the Fed by virtue of its enormous capital resources. The true center of power within the Fed is the Federal Open Market Committee (FOMC), on which only the NY Fed President holds a permanent voting seat. The FOMC issues directives on monetary policy which are implemented from the 8th

Floor of the NY Fed, a fortress modeled after the Bank of England. [68] In the fifth sub-basement of the 14-story stone hulk lie 10,300 tons of mostly non-US gold, 1/3 of the world's gold reserves and by far the largest gold stock in the world. [69]

The world of money is increasingly computerized. With the introduction of complicated financial instruments like derivatives, options, puts and futures; the volume of inter-bank transactions took a quantum leap. To handle this the fed built a superhighway eerily known as CHIPS (Clearing Interbank Payment System), which is based in New York and modeled after Morgan's Belgium-based Euro-Clear, also known as The Beast.

When the Fed was created five New York banks - Citibank, Chase, Chemical Bank, Manufacturers Hanover and Bankers Trust - held a 43% stake in the New York Fed. By 1983 these same five banks owned 53% of the NY Fed. By year 2000, the newly merged Citigroup, JP Morgan Chase and Deutsche Bank combines owned even bigger chunks. The remainder is owned by the European faction of the Eight Families. Collectively they own majority stock in every Fortune 500 corporation and do the bulk of stock and bond trading. In 1955 the above five banks accounted for 15% of all stock trades. By 1985 they were involved in 85% of all stock transactions. [70]

Still more powerful are the investment banks which bear the names of many of the Eight Families. In 1982, while Morgan bankers presided over negotiations between Britain and Argentina after the Falklands War, President Reagan pushed through SEC Rule 415, which helped consolidate securities underwriting in the hands of six large investment houses owned by the Eight Families: Goldman Sachs, Merrill Lynch, Morgan Stanley, Salomon Brothers, First Boston and Lehman Brothers. These banks further consolidated their power *via* the merger mania of 1980s and 1990s.

American Express swallowed up both Lehman Brothers-Kuhn Loeb, which had merged in 1977, and Shearson Lehman-Rhoades. The Israel Moses Seif's *Banca de la Svizzera Italiana* bought a 7% stake in Lehman Brothers. [71] Salomon Brothers nabbed Philbro from the South African Oppenheimer family, then bought Smith Barney. All three then became part of Traveler's Group, headed by Sandy Weill of the David-Weill family, which controls Lazard

Freres through senior partner Michel David-Weill. Citibank then bought Travelers to form Citigroup. S.G. Warburg, of which Oppenheimer's Chartered Consolidated owns a 9% stake, joined the old money *Banque Pariba*s - which merged into Merrill Lynch in 1984. Union Bank of Switzerland acquired Paine Webber, while Morgan Stanley ate up Dean Witter and purchased Discover credit card operations from Sears.

Kuhn Loeb-controlled First Boston merged with Credit Suisse, which had already absorbed White-Weld, to become CS First Boston - the major player in the dirty London Eurobond market. Merrill Lynch - merged into Bank of America in 2008 - is the major player on the US side of this trade. Swiss Banking Corporation merged with London's biggest investment house S.G. Warburg to create SBC Warburg, while Warburg became more intertwined with Merrill Lynch through their 1998 Mercury Assets tie up. The Warburg's formed another venture with Union Bank of Switzerland, creating powerhouse UBS Warburg. Deutsche Bank bought Banker's Trust and Alex Brown to become the world's largest bank with $882 billion in assets. With repeal of Glass-Steagal, the line between investment, commercial and private banking disappeared.

This handful of investment banks exerts an enormous amount of control over the global economy. Their activities include advising Third World debt negotiations, handling mergers and breakups, creating companies to fill a perceived economic void through the launching of initial public stock offerings (IPOs), underwriting all stocks, underwriting all corporate and government bond issuance, and pulling the bandwagon down the road of privatization and globalization of the world economy. The current president of the World Bank is James Wolfensohn of Salomon Smith Barney. Merrill Lynch had $435 billion in assets in 1994, before the merger frenzy had really even gotten under way. The biggest commercial bank at the time, Citibank, could claim only $249 billion in assets.

In 1991 Merrill Lynch handled 26.8% of all global bank mergers. Morgan Stanley did 16.8%, Goldman Sachs 16.3%, Lehman Brothers 16.1% and Credit Suisse First Boston 14.5%. Morgan Stanley did $60 billion in corporate mergers in 1989. By 2007, reflecting the repeal of Glass-Steagel, the top ten NMA advisers in order were: Goldman Sachs, Morgan Stanley, Citigroup,

JP Morgan Chase, Lehman Brothers, Merrill Lynch, UBS Warburg, Credit Suisse, Deutsche Bank and Lazard. In the IPO stock underwriting field for 1991 the top four were Goldman Sachs, Merrill Lynch, Morgan Stanley and CS First Boston. In the arena of global privatization for years 1985-1995, Goldman Sachs led the way doing $13.3 billion worth of deals. UBS Warburg did $8.2 billion, BNP *Paribas* $6.8 billion, CS First Boston $4.9 billion and *Paribas*-owner Merrill Lynch $4.4 billion. [72] In 2006 BNP *Paribas* bought the notorious *Banca Nacionale de Lavoro* (BNL).

The leading US debt underwriters for the first nine months of 1995 bore the same familiar names. Merrill Lynch underwrote $74.2 billion in the US debt markets, or 15.3% of the total. Lehman Brothers handled $52.5 billion, Morgan Stanley $47.4 billion, Salomon Smith Barney $45.6 billion. CS First Boston, Chase Manhattan and Goldman Sachs rounded out the top seven. The top three municipal debt underwriters that year were Goldman Sachs, Merrill Lynch and UBS Paine Webber. In the euro-market the top four underwriters in 1995 were UBS Warburg, Merrill Lynch, Deutsche Bank and Goldman Sachs. [73] Deutsche Bank's Morgan Grenfell branch engineered the corporate takeover binge in Europe.

The dominant players in the oil futures markets at both the New York Mercantile Exchange and the London Petroleum Exchange are Morgan Stanley Dean Witter, Goldman Sachs (through its J. Aron & Company subsidiary), Citigroup (through its Philbro unit) and Deutsche Bank (through its Banker's Trust acquisition). In 2002 Enron Online was auctioned off by a bankruptcy court to UBS Warburg for $0. UBS was to share monopoly Enron Online profits with Lehman Brothers after the first two years of the deal. [74] With Lehman's 2008 demise, Barclays will get their cut.

Following the Lehman Brothers fiasco and the ensuing financial meltdown of 2008, the Four Horsemen of Banking got even bigger. For pennies on the dollar, JP Morgan Chase was handed Bear Stearns and Washington Mutual. Bank of America commandeered Merrill Lynch and Countrywide. And Wells Fargo seized control over the reeling #5 US bank Wachovia. Barclays got a sweetheart deal for the remains of Lehman Brothers.

House Banking Committee Chairman Wright Patman (D-TX), declared of Federal Reserve Eight Families owners, "The United

States today has in effect two governments. We are the duly constituted government. Then we have an independent, uncontrolled and uncoordinated government in the Federal Reserve System, operating the money powers which are reserved to Congress by the Constitution". [75]

Since the creation of the Federal Reserve, US debt to the Eight Families has skyrocketed: from $1 billion to over $13 trillion today. This far surpasses the total of all Third World country debt combined, debt which is also owed to these same Eight Families who own most all the world's central banks.

As Sen. Barry Goldwater (R-AZ) pointed out, "International bankers make money by extending credit to governments. The greater the debt of the political state, the larger the interest returned to lenders. The national banks of Europe are (also) owned and controlled by private interests. We recognize in a hazy sort of way that the Rothschilds and the Warburgs of Europe and the houses of JP Morgan, Kuhn Loeb & Co., Schiff, Lehman and Rockefeller possess and control vast wealth. How they acquire this vast financial power and employ it is a mystery to most of us."[76]

The Solution

Thomas Jefferson opined of the Rothschild-led Eight Families central banking cartel which came to control the United States, "Single acts of tyranny may be ascribed to the accidental opinion of the day, but a series of oppressions begun at a distinguished period, unalterable through every change of ministers, too plainly prove a deliberate, systematic plan of reducing us to slavery".

Two centuries and a few decades later this same cabal of trillionaire money changers - mysteriously immune from their own calls for "broad sacrifice" - utilizes the debt lever to ring concessions from the people of Ireland, Greece, Spain, Portugal, Italy and now the United States.

In their never-ending quest to subjugate the planet, the bankers' IMF enforcer - chronic harasser of Third World governments - has turned its sites on the developed world. To further advance their dizzying concentration of economic power, the whining banksters take a giant wrecking ball to the global middle class as they prepare to eat their young.

No one can argue that the US deficit is not a problem. Much of it accrues paying interest on the $17 trillion debt. Stooped-over Congressional cartel shills with names like Cantor and Boehner argue for slashing entire government departments to satiate the bloodthirsty bond-holders. Liberals argue for higher taxes on the rich and massive Pentagon cuts.

I agree with these latter proposals. The super-rich paid 90% under Eisenhower and 72% under Nixon. Both were Republicans. They now pay 33%. Most corporations and many elites utilize offshore tax havens and pay nothing.

The argument for progressive taxation is that those who benefit more from government should pay more. Cartel apologists propagate the fiction that the poor soak up middle-class tax dollars, sowing division between the poor and middle class. Meanwhile, the Eight Families financial octopus feeds mightily at the public trough be it the SEC (rich investors), the FCC (Gulfstream jet fliers), the USDA (the richest farmers get the biggest checks), Medicaid (insurance fraud, Big Pharma gouging) or the Pentagon (Lockheed Martin, Halliburton, Blackwater).

Still, $17 trillion is an insurmountable debt. Increasing taxes on the super-rich combined with a global American military withdrawal from its current role as *Hessianized* mercenary force for the City of London banksters, while welcome, will not be enough to deal with this monster debt, what Jefferson termed, this "deliberate, systematic plan of reducing us to slavery".

The belt-way dialogue on the deficit remains locked in a tiny intellectual box created by the corporate media and their Federal Reserve cartel owners. But there is another way.

It is a myth that most of that $17 trillion debt is owed to the Chinese or other "governments". The vast majority - around $13 trillion - is owed to the Eight Families Federal Reserve crowd.

In a June 9, 2011 article for *Marketwatch*, Unicredit's Chief US Economist Harm Bandholz stated that the Federal Reserve is the largest holder of US debt with around 14% of the total. This does not include debt held by Rothschild-controlled central banks of *other* nations - including China, Japan and the GCC oil fiefdoms.

Through the recent QE2 and QE3 programs, the Fed purchased another $2 trillion in Treasury bonds. They claimed it was a last ditch attempt to save the global economy from deflation. Instead, the banksters who got the interest free taxpayer-backed money pushed us further *towards* deflation by refusing to lend their welfare bonanza to potential homeowners or small business.

Conversely and inherent in the printing of zero-interest money, they also created inflation - speculating in oil, food and gold futures and rolling this increased US debt on the roulette tables at their various wholly-owned global stock exchanges. Is it any wonder the financial parasite class is now clamoring for QE4?

What follows is a ten-step proposal which President Obama and the Congress could enact to lift the $17 trillion debt from the backs of future generations of Americans. These should be done concurrently as part of a single sweeping financial reform bill. These measures should be enacted in tandem with as many willing nations as possible.

The same Rothschild-led cabal controls the central banks of most every nation and there is power in numbers. If these measures are enacted separately or by only one nation, the Eight Families' cartel will use their financial clout to target and destroy the US:

1) Introduce a Treasury Department-administered infrastructure investment fund, which workers should be strongly encouraged to opt into using accrued funds from their private 401K plans. This is important because the banker's stock market casino *will* crash due to the next nine steps and workers must be shielded from this event. This fund can be used to rebuild America's infrastructure, with American workers acting as lenders and receiving a fair rate of interest in return.

2) The US needs to withdraw from the Bank of International Settlements, the World Trade Organization, the World Bank, the IMF and all Eight Families-controlled multilateral lending facilities. We would save billions funding these banker welfare schemes while freeing ourselves from rules which prevent our financial emancipation.

3) De-link the dollar from all currency baskets and IMF special drawing rights. Ban trade in dollars on all global exchanges. This will create a demand for dollars and strengthen our badly devalued currency. Impose currency controls by fixing the dollar at 1:1 *euro*, Chinese *yuan*, Canadian dollar and Swiss *franc*; 100:1 Japanese *yen*. During the 1997 Asian financial crisis, Malaysian Prime Minister Mahathir Mohamad fixed the nation's currency - the *ringit*. It was the only currency in the region that did not crash when Rothschild front-man George Soros took aim at the region.

4) Nationalize the Federal Reserve. According to a London barrister I have been in contact with, under the Federal Reserve Act there is a provision that allows for the US government to buy back the Fed's charter for $4 billion. We should pay this fee, revoke the Fed charter and launch a new US dollar issued by the Treasury Department. With the dollar fixed, the vampires cannot crash it.

5) Cancel the $13 trillion debt to the *Illuminati* bankers. Debt obligations to foreign governments and small bond-holders should be honored at par.

6) Arrest the perpetrators. Prosecute to the fullest extent of the law all fraudulent transactions involving the Fed cartel. Send the FBI to the New York Fed. Seize all documents. Confiscate the world's largest gold reserves which are stored there. These were stolen from various governments including from our own Ft. Knox reserves.

7) Forget just repealing the Bush tax cuts on the rich. The top tax rate on people who make more than $1 million/year should be raised to 75%. People making more than $500,000/year should pay 50%. All tax brackets below $75,000/year should see tax *cuts*. If you get more from government you need to pay for it, instead of soaking the middle-class and blaming it on the poor.

8) Slash Pentagon spending. Shut down all US military bases on foreign soil, including those in Europe, Japan and South Korea. Withdraw ALL troops from Iraq and Afghanistan immediately. Use the savings to pay off government and small bond-holders.

9) Outlaw offshore banking by US citizens and corporations. Bring your money home and pay taxes on it or surrender your US passport and corporate charter. The dramatic increase in tax revenue would be enough to pay off the remaining debt to sovereign governments and small bond-holders, while keeping our obligations to the Social Security trust fund.

10) Introduce single-payer health care and price controls on prescription drugs. The current corporate for-profit health care bonanza depends upon sickness and ill health for its hefty profits. In 2006 Canada government spent $3,678 per person for free single-payer coverage for all its citizens. The US government spent $6,714 per person covering the insurance, pharmaceutical, hospital and AMA cartels. The savings attained from eliminating current rampant insurance/pharmaceutical/hospital chain/doctor-perpetrated Medicare/Medicaid/Social Security fraud will save the US Treasury billions. It is the only solution to skyrocketing and unsustainable health care costs.

Using this methodology the US could wipe out both its deficit and its debt within a year. These measures should be planned in secret and introduced swiftly and in rapid succession. Social security and Medicare will be saved. The middle class will see their tax rates go down, while their new retirement fund finances the rebuilding of a 21st Century America. Manufacturing jobs will come home, since the Chinese *yuan* will have seen a dramatic appreciation. Our national security will be enhanced by withdrawing from the role of global policeman.

If we keep thinking inside the banker-manufactured beltway box, our children have no future. They will live in a Third World country which produces nothing, lorded over by debt-collector parasites known as the "financial services industry".

The wealth-destroying Eight Families banker elite are the perpetrators of the US debt crime. Should a woman who is raped serve the sentence of her rapist? That's absurd. Then why should Americans or the people of any other nation pay a fraudulent debt foisted upon them by con-men?

It is time for Obama and the Congress to get a backbone and force the criminal Federal Reserve cartel to make the "broad sacrifices". The only way this will happen is if the American people unite around this issue and make nationalizing the Federal Reserve the rallying cry of the new American Revolution.

Footnotes

[1] 10K Filings of Fortune 500 Corporations to SEC. 3-91

[2] 10K Filing of US Trust Corporation to SEC. 6-28-95

[3] "The Federal Reserve 'Fed Up'. Thomas Schauf. www.davidicke.com 1-02

[4] *The Secrets of the Federal Reserve*. Eustace Mullins. Bankers Research Institute. Staunton, VA. 1983. p.179

[5] Ibid. p.53

[6] *The Triumph of Conservatism*. Gabriel Kolko. MacMillan and Company New York. 1963. p.142

[7] *Rule by Secrecy: The Hidden History that Connects the Trilateral Commission, the Freemasons and the Great Pyramids*. Jim Marrs. HarperCollins Publishers. New York. 2000. p.57

[8] *The House of Morgan*. Ron Chernow. Atlantic Monthly Press NewYork 1990

[9] Marrs. p.57

[10] *Democracy for the Few*. Michael Parenti. St. Martin's Press. New York. 1977. p.178

[11] Chernow

[12] *The Great Crash of 1929*. John Kenneth Galbraith. Houghton, Mifflin Company. Boston. 1979. p.148

[13] Chernow

[14] Children of the Matrix. David Icke. Bridge of Love. Scottsdale, AZ. 2000

[15] *The Confidence Game: How Un-Elected Central Bankers are Governing the Changed World Economy*. Steven Solomon. Simon & Schuster. New York. 1995. p.112

[16] Marrs. p.180

[17] Ibid. p.45

[18] *The Money Lenders: The People and Politics of the World Banking Crisis*. Anthony Sampson. Penguin Books. New York. 1981

[19] *The Rockefeller File*. Gary Allen. '76 Press. Seal Beach, CA. 1977

[20] Ibid

[21] *The Rockefeller Syndrome*. Ferdinand Lundberg. Lyle Stuart Inc. Secaucus, NJ. 1975. p.296

[22] Marrs. p.53

[23] *The Temple and the Lodge*. Michael Bagent and Richard Leigh. Arcade Publishing. New York. 1989. p.259

[24] Ibid. p.219

[25] Ibid. p.253

[26] Ibid. p.233

[27] The *Robot's Rebellion: The Story of the Spiritual Renaissance*. David Icke. Gateway Books. Bath, UK. 1994. p.156

[28] Parenti. p.51

[29] *Fourth Reich of the Rich*. Des Griffin. Emissary Publications. Pasadena, CA. 1978. p.171

[30] Ibid. p.173

[31] Marrs. p.68

[32] Mullins

[33] Marrs. p.212

[34] Icke. 1994. p.114

[35] Ibid. p.181

[36] *Rothschild: The Wealth and Power of a Dynasty*. Derek Wilson. Charles Schribner's Sons. New York. 1988. p.178

[37] *The House of Rothschild*. Niall Ferguson. Viking Press New York 1998 p.28

[38] Marrs. p.215

[39] "What You Didn't Know about Taxes and the Crown". Mark Owen. *Paranoia*. #41. Spring 2006. p.66

[40] Marrs. p.63

[41] "The Secret Financial Network Behind 'Wizard' George Soros". William Engdahl. *Executive Intelligence Review*. 11-1-96

[42] Marrs. p.80

[43] Engdahl

[44] Marrs. p.83

[45] Ibid. p.89

[46] Griffin. p.77

[47] Icke. 1994. p.195

[48] *Dope Inc.: The Book that Drove Kissinger Crazy*. The Editors of *Executive Intelligence Review*. Washington, DC. 1992. p.264

[49] Ibid. p.538

[50] Icke. 1994. p.148

[51] Ibid

[52] *Behold a Pale Horse*. William Cooper. Light Technology Press. Sedona, AZ. 1991. p.79

[53] Icke. 2000.

[54] Marrs. p.71

[55] Icke. 1996. p.42

[56] Ibid. p.71

[57] Cooper

[58] Ibid. p.81

[59] Parenti. p.67

[60] *Descent into Slavery*. Des Griffin. Emissary Publications. Pasadena 1991

[61] Icke. 1994. p.158

[62] The Editors of *Executive Intelligence Review*. p.504

[63] Ibid

[64] Ibid

[65] Ibid. p.77

[66] "Secrets of the Federal Reserve". Discovery Channel. January 2002

[67] Solomon. p.26

[68] Icke. p.178

[69] Solomon. p.63

[70] Ibid. p.27

[71] *The Corporate Reapers: The Book of Agribusiness*. A.V. Krebs. Essential Books. Washington, DC. 1992. p.166

[72] The Editors of *Executive Intelligence Review*. p.79

[73] "Playing the Middle". Anita Raghavan and Bridget O'Brian. *Wall Street Journal*. 10-2-95

[74] Securities Data Corporation. 1995

[75] CNN Headline News. 1-11-02

[76] Allen. p.156

About the Author

Dean Henderson was born in Faulkton, South Dakota. He earned a BLS at the University of South Dakota and an MS in Environmental Studies from the University of Montana where he edited The Missoula Paper and was a columnist for the Montana Kaimin. His articles have appeared in Multinational Monitor, In These Times, Paranoia and hundreds of online websites and magazines.

A life-long activist and traveler to over 50 countries, Henderson appears regularly as a political analyst for Iran's Press TV, RT, Russian Channel 1, The Syria Times, Rense Radio,Tactical Talk with Zain Khan and The Richie Allen Show. In June 2018, Dean spoke at New York City's Deep Truth conference where he delivered a speech titled, "All Roads Lead to the City of London" as part of a panel named Confronting Oligarchy: Resisting Full Spectrum Dominance.

Dean and his wife Jill live in the Missouri Ozarks where the rivers run clear, the water tastes sweet, and the air is clean. They operate and live on a small organic vegetable farm, burn wood for heat, and gather wild berries, mushrooms, fruits and nuts. They don't work slave wage jobs and buy very little, living a simple and rich life.

Subscribe free to Dean's weekly column and interviews at
HendersonLeftHook.wordpress.com

Other Books by Dean Henderson

Big Oil & Their Bankers in the Persian Gulf
*Four Horsemen, Eight Families & Their Global
Narcotics & Terror Network*
An internationally acclaimed best-seller that started the recent
conversation about who really runs the world, Big Oil... exposes a
centuries-old cabal of global oligarchs that control the global
economy through manipulation of the world's central banks via the
planet's three most valuable commodities: oil, guns and drugs.

Stickin' It to the Matrix
Stickin' it to the Matrix is this generation's version of Abbie
Hoffman's Steal This Book. Funny and irreverent, it is above all a
practical step-by-step guide to both escaping and extracting from the
matrix. In Stickin' it to the Matrix, Henderson offers the reader the
same insights that allowed him to "retire" at age 28, move to the
country and author this and other books.

The Grateful Unrich
Revolution in 50 Countries
Covering fifty countries on six continents over a twenty-year span,
Henderson asks the hard social, political and economic questions
while vagabonding his way around the world. Invoking the wit and
humor of Twain and the curiosity of Kerouac, Henderson discovers
himself, humanity and revolutionary politics through prolonged
contact with God's chosen people - The Grateful Unrich.

Illuminati Agenda 21
The Luciferian Plan to Destroy Creation
This is the story of the age- old battle between Good and Evil
beginning with the Luciferian perpetrators, tracing their origins to
ancient Sumeria and tracking their hegemony over mankind through
Babylon, Egypt, the Holy Roman Empire and their modern-day

Masonic lair: The City of London. Here, the Illuminati's Agenda 21 quietly unfolds in an insidious creep towards global fascism and a New World Secular Order, which threatens to strip us of our humanity, replace us with machines, and destroy all Creation.

Nephilim Crown 5G Apocalypse

Nephilim Crown 5G Apocalypse is an indictment of the computer revolution as the latest mechanism through which royal bloodline families seek to control humanity. The roll out of their battlefield 5G weapons system represents the pinnacle in their use of electromagnetic frequencies to literally remote control their human herd. Since their intervention in Sumeria, these hybrid fallen angel Nephilim have usurped, steered, and plundered all of Creation as self-appointed god kings. The coming 5G apocalypse represents a great unveiling of not only their nefarious 5G deception, but of the fraudulent Nephilim Crown itself.

Printed in Poland
by Amazon Fulfillment
Poland Sp. z o.o., Wrocław